# ألف ليلة وليلة

## للمبتدئين بتعلم
## اللغة العربية اللبنانية

# One Thousand and One Nights

## for Elementary Levantine Arabic Language Learners

lingualism

© 2023 by Matthew Aldrich

The author's moral rights have been asserted. All rights reserved. No part of this document may be reproduced or transmitted in any form or by any means, electronic, mechanical, photocopying, recording, or otherwise, without prior written permission of the publisher.

ISBN: 978-1-949650-96-9

Conceptualized by Matthew Aldrich

Written by Ahmad Al-Masri

Translated (from Egyptian Arabic to Lebanese Arabic) by Charbel Ghaleb

Edited by Matthew Aldrich

Illustrations by Duc-Minh Vu

Audio by Charbel Ghaleb

website: www.lingualism.com

email: contact@lingualism.com

# Table of Contents

II ............................................................ INTRODUCTION

V ................................................. HOW TO USE THIS BOOK

1 ............................................. الفَصْل الأوّل: الوَزير وبِنتو والمَلِك
Chapter 1: The Vizier, His Daughter, and the King

8 ................................................ الفَصْل الثّاني: الجِنّي والتّاجِر
Chapter 2: The Genie and the Merchant

17 ............................................ الفَصْل الثّالِت: الصّيّاد والسَّمَكة الذَّهبية
Chapter 3: The Fisherman and the Golden Fish

25 .................................... الفَصْل الرّابع: علاء الدّين والمِصباح السِّحري
Chapter 4: Aladdin and the Magic Lamp

34 ......................................... الفَصْل الخامِس: علي بابا والأرْبعين حرامي
Chapter 5: Ali Baba and the Forty Thieves

41 ................................. الفَصْل السّادِس: الفِلّاح الذَّكي والجِنّي الشَّقي
Chapter 6: The Clever Farmer and the Mischievous Genie

49 ......................................... الفَصْل السّابع: حرامي إسْكنْدرية ورئيس الشُّرْطة
Chapter 7: The Thief of Alexandria and the Police Chief

57 ......................................................... الفَصْل الثّامِن: العُصْفور الأزْرق
Chapter 8: The Blue Bird

65 ................................................. الفَصْل التّاسِع: البِنْت والسّاحِرة الخْتيارة
Chapter 9: The Girl and the Magical Old Woman

72 ....................................................... الفَصْل العاشِر: الأمير والتِّنين
Chapter 10: The Prince and the Dragon

# Introduction

"One Thousand and One Nights for Elementary Levantine Arabic Language Learners" is a captivating anthology designed specifically for adult Arabic language learners at the elementary level. This unique collection features the cherished classic tales in a simplified, yet engaging format, making it an excellent resource for those venturing into the enchanting world of Arabic language and literature.

The book comes with an array of special features to ensure an immersive and effective learning experience:

- **Diacritics for Pronunciation:** We've included diacritical marks (tashkeel) in the Arabic text to assist you in correct pronunciation, and to clarify the meaning of the words, easing your reading experience.

- **Professional Audio Accompaniment:** The book is supplemented with high-quality, slow-paced audio readings by a professional voice artist who is a native Arabic speaker from Lebanon. This allows you to listen and mimic the correct pronunciation, intonation, and rhythm of Levantine Arabic.

- **Comprehension Questions and Answers:** Each chapter is followed by a set of comprehension questions, along with their answers. This interactive feature helps to reinforce your understanding of the story and the language constructs used within it.

- **English Translations:** To support your learning, we've provided English translations of the stories. These can be used as a reference to cross-check your understanding of the Arabic text.

All these features work together to provide a comprehensive and enriching learning experience, ensuring you make consistent progress in your Arabic language journey.

The tales in this book have been carefully curated and reimagined to match the language proficiency of elementary-level learners. We have incorporated level-appropriate vocabulary throughout the stories, ensuring you are neither overwhelmed by complexity nor left unchallenged. To enhance memorization and recognition, we've deliberately woven repetitive patterns of phrases and language structures into the text, encouraging natural language acquisition and recall.

Each chapter is short, and perfectly crafted to be absorbed in a single sitting, allowing you to steadily build your comprehension skills and vocabulary without feeling rushed. The stories retain the intrigue and charm of the original tales, providing you with a sense of accomplishment and enjoyment as you navigate your way through each tale.

Once you've mastered the stories and vocabulary in this book, we invite you to progress to the "One Thousand and One Nights for <u>Intermediate</u> Levantine Arabic Language Learners." In this next step of your language journey, you'll find the same beloved stories, but presented in slightly different versions. These alternate renditions are imbued with greater detail, building on the vocabulary you learn in this book, and introducing you to new vocabulary and more nuanced language structures. This ensures a smooth, seamless transition towards more advanced language learning.

With "One Thousand and One Nights for Elementary Levantine Arabic Language Learners," not only will you embark on a remarkable journey through some of the most enchanting stories ever told, but you'll also be laying a strong and solid foundation for your Arabic language learning adventure.

# How to Use This Book

"One Thousand and One Nights for Elementary Levantine Arabic Language Learners" has been designed to offer flexibility to adapt to your individual learning style. Here's how you can utilize the features of the book according to your needs:

1. **Choose Your Approach:** You have the freedom to approach the stories in multiple ways. You could begin by tackling the Arabic text first, immersing yourself in the structure of the language and the flow of the story. Alternatively, you could start by listening to the accompanying audio, to attune your ear to the sound and rhythm of Levantine Arabic. This can be particularly helpful if you are a more auditory learner.
2. **Use English Translations:** If you're finding the Arabic text or audio challenging, you can refer to the English translations to aid your understanding. Over time, as your comprehension improves, you could challenge yourself by attempting to read or listen to the Arabic without relying on the translations.
3. **Engage with Questions:** You can choose to tackle the comprehension questions before or after reading the story. Attempting them beforehand can provide a focus for your reading, while answering them after

allows you to assess your understanding of the text. Remember, the answers provided in the book are examples and your own answers, while differently worded, may still be correct.

4. **Repetition and Practice:** This book has been designed to promote repetition and practice, key strategies for language learning. We encourage you to revisit chapters and listen to the audio multiple times to reinforce your understanding and memorization.

Remember, the most effective learning strategy is the one that works best for you. So don't be afraid to experiment with different approaches until you find what suits you best.

Visit www.lingualism.com/audio, where you can find the free accompanying audio to download or stream (at variable playback rates).

# الفَصْل الأوّل
# الوَزير وبِنْتو والمَلِك

بِيوْم مِن الإيّام، بِبلد بْعيد، كان في مَلِك حكيم وعادِل إسمو شهْرَيار. كان بْيِحْكُم مَمْلِكة كْبيرة، وشعْبو كان بيحِبّو كْتير.

بِقصُر المَلِك، كان في زلمي حكيم إسْمو جعْفر وكان هُوَّ الوَزير. كان بيساعِد المَلِك بِالْقرارات الْمُهِمَّة. جعْفر كان زلمي طيِّب ومُخْلِص، وكان عنْدو بِنت حِلْوة إسما شهرزاد.

شهْرزاد كانِت بِنت ذكية وشُجاعة. كانِت بِتْحِبّ تِقرا وتِتْعلّم شغَلات عن الدّني. كانِت بْتعْرِف قُصص كْتير وبتعْرِف تْخبّرا بِطريقة تْخلّي النّاس تْحِبّ تِسْمعا.

بِيوْم مِن الإيّام، قرّر المِلِك شهْرَيار إنّو يِتْجوّز. طلب مِن وَزيرو يْنبّشْلو على عروس. نبّش جعْفر كْتير بسّ ما قِدِر يْلاقي عروس مُناسْبة للمِلِك.

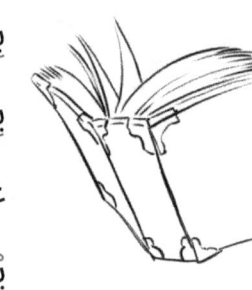

فجْأة، خطرِت فِكْرة لشهْرزاد. راحِت لعِنْد بيّا الوَزير وقالِتْلو: "يا بابا، أنا بدّي كون مرْة المِلِك. أنا عِنْدي كْتير قُصص خبّرو ياها. وبإقْدر إسْعِدو."

الوَزير كان قلْقان على بِنْتو. كان عارِف إنّو المِلِك شهْرَيار مُمْكِن يْعصّب أوْقات. بسّ شهْرزاد كانِت مُصِرّة إنّا تِتْجوّز المِلِك.

و كِرْمال هيْك، وافِق الوَزير على الجازة. وخبّرو للمِلِك شهْرَيار عن بِنْتو، والمِلِك وافِق يِتْجوّزا.

بِليْلِة عِرْسُن، بلّشِت شهْرزاد تْخبّر للمِلِك قُصّة. كانِت القُصّة

حِلْوِة كْتير لدرجِة إنّو المَلِك كان بدّو إنّو تْخبّرو بعِد. قالِتْلو شهْرزاد: "أنا حكمِّل القُصّة بُكرا باللّيْل لَوْ سمحْتِلي." وافق المَلِك شهْرَيار على طلبا، وكان بدّو يِسمع كْتير قُصص كمان.

و هيْك، بلّشِت شهْرزاد تْخبّر القُصص للْمَلِك شهْرَيار كِلّ ليْلِة. كانِت القُصص مِليانة مُغامرات وغُموض وحُبّ. كان المَلِك مِتحمِّس إنّو يِسْمع كِلّ قُصّة جْديدِة وكان يِتْعلّم مِنّا شغْلات كْتير عن الحَياةْ والدّني.

## Questions

1. شو إِسِم المِلِك الحكيم العادِل؟

2. شو الشغْلِة اللي كانِت شهْرزاد بِتْحِبّ تعْمِلا؟

3. شو يلّي طلبو المِلِك شهْرَيار مِن وَزيرو جعْفر؟

4. كيف شهْرزاد تْعرّفِت على المِلِك شهْرَيار؟

5. شو الشّغْلِة اللي بلّشِت شهْرزاد تعْمِلا كِلّ ليْلِة بعْد ما تْجوّزِت المِلِك شهْرَيار؟

## Answers

1. إسْم المِلك هُوّ شهْرَيار.

2. كانِت شهْرزاد بِتْحِبّ تِقْرا وتِتْعلّم قُصص عن الدّني، وكانِت بْتعْرِف قُصص كْتير، وبْتعْرِف تخبّرا.

3. طلب المِلك شهْرَيار مِن وَزيرو جعْفر إنّو يُنبّشلو على عروس.

4. راحِت شهْرزاد لعِنْد بيّا الوَزير وقالِتْلو إنّا بدّا تْكون مرْة المِلك، وبعْديْن الوَزير قال لِلْمِلك عن بِنْتو والمِلك وافق إنّو يِتْجوّزا.

5. بلّشِت شهْرزاد تْخبّر قُصص لِلْملِك شهْرَيار كِلّ ليْلة.

## Chapter 1: The Vizier, His Daughter, and the King

Once upon a time, in a faraway land, there was a wise and just king named Shahryar. He ruled a great kingdom and was loved by his people.

In the king's court, there was a wise man named Ja'far, who was the vizier. He helped the king make important decisions. Ja'far was a kind and loyal man, and he had a beautiful daughter named Scheherazade.

Scheherazade was a intelligent, brave girl. She loved reading and learning about the world. She knew many stories and could tell them in a way that made people listen.

One day, King Shahryar decided that he needed a queen. He asked his vizier to find him a wife. Ja'far searched for a long time but could not find a suitable wife for the king.

Scheherazade had an idea. She went to her father, the vizier, and said, "Father, I want to be the king's wife. I have many stories to tell him. I can make him happy."

The vizier was worried about his daughter. He knew that King Shahryar could get very angry sometimes. But Scheherazade was determined to marry the king.

So the vizier agreed to the marriage. He told King Shahryar about his daughter, and the king agreed to marry her.

On their wedding night, Scheherazade began to tell the king a story. The story was so interesting that the king wanted to hear more. Scheherazade said, "I will finish the story tomorrow night if you allow me." King Shahryar agreed and wanted to hear more stories.

And so Scheherazade began to tell stories to King Shahryar every night. The stories were full of adventures, mysteries, and love. The king was eager to hear every new story and learned a lot about life and the world from them.

Questions
1. What is the name of the wise and just king?
2. What did Scheherazade love to do?
3. What did King Shahryar ask his vizier Ja'far to do?
4. How did Scheherazade meet King Shahryar?
5. What did Scheherazade begin to do every night after marrying King Shahryar?

Answers
1. The name of the king is Shahryar.
2. Scheherazade loved reading and learning about the world, and she knew many stories that she could tell.
3. King Shahryar asked his vizier Ja'far to find him a wife.
4. Scheherazade went to her father, the vizier, and said she wanted to be the king's wife, so the vizier told the king about his daughter, and the king agreed to marry her.
5. Scheherazade began to tell stories to King Shahryar every night.

# الفصل التّاني
## الجِنّي والتّاجِر

بِاللّيْلِة اللي بعْدا، طلب المِلك شهْريار مِن شهرزاد إنّا تْخبّرو قُصّة جْديدِة. فا بلّشِت شهرزاد تِحْكي قُصّة التّاجِر والجِنّي العجيب.

بِيوْم مِن الإيّام، سافر تاجِر غني بِرِحْلِة بْعيدِة كِرمال يْبيع بْضاعْتو. بعْد رِحْلِة طويلِة ومِتْعِبة، وِقِف التّاجِر كِرمال يِرْتاح

تحِت شجرة. وهُوَّ وقاعِد هونيك، ظهر جِنّي عِمْلاق ومْعصّب.

قال الجنّي للتّاجِر: "أنا حإقْتِلك لأنّو إنْتَ دمّرتِلّي بَيْتي." التّاجِر كان خايِف ومِش فاهِم الجِنّي شو قصْدو. طلب مِن الجِنّي يِفهّمو هُوَّ ليْش مْعصّب.

فا ردّ الجِنّي: "لمّا إنْتَ جيت وشِلْت جِذِع الخشب هَيْدا كِرمال تُقْعُد عْليْه، وَقّعْت عْليّي شغْلات دمّرت بَيْتي الصّغير اللي كِنت عايِش فيه."

كان التّاجِر زِعْلان بِسبب يَلّي صار، بسّ هُوَّ مكان عارِف إنّو في بيْت جِنّي وَرا الشّجرة. طلب مِن الجِنّي إنّو يْكون رحوم ويْسامْحو.

قال الجِنّي: "أنا رح أعْطيك فُرْصة تْجيب حدا يِقْنعْني إنّي ما إقْتلك. وإذا فْشِلِت، أكيد حتْموت."

راح التّاجِر بِرِحْلة طَويلة يْدوّر على حدا يْساعْدو. بالآخر، لِقي زلمي خِتيار حكيم كان بْيَعْرِف خبْريات كْتيرة عن الجِنّ وعالمُن.

سِمع الرِّجال الخِتْيار قُصّة التّاجِر وقرّر إنّو يْساعْدو. راحوا سَوا لمطرح الشّجرة اللي كان الجِنّي ناطْرُن عِندا.

قال الرِّجال الخِتْيار للْجِنّي: "أنا بدّي خبْرك قُصّة قبِل ما تْقرّر مصير هَيدا التّاجِر. لَوْ عجبِتك القُصّة، بِتْمنّى إنّك تْسامْحو وتْخلّي يْعيش."

وافق الجِنّي إنّو يِسْمع القُصّة. بلّش الخِتْيار يْخبّر قُصّة مُشوّقة عن المُغامرة والشّجاعة والتّضحية. كانِت القُصّة مِلْيانة تِشْويق ودْروس مْهِمّة.

بَعد ما سِمع الجِنّي القُصّة، قال: "القُصّة عجبِتْني كتير وتْعلّمِت مِنّا دْروس عظيمة. أنا حسامِح التّاجِر ومِش حإقِتْلو، بِشرِط يِنْتِبِهْ إنّو ما يْعيد هيْك غلْطة مرّة تانْية."

شكر التّاجِر الجِنّي على رحِمْتو، ووَعد إنّو حينْتِبِهْ عَ تصرُّفاتو. وكمان شكر الرِّجال الخِتْيار على مُساعِدْتو وحِكْمْتو. بَعْديْن، رِجع التّاجِر لضيْعْتو وعيْلْتو ووَعد إنّو حَيْكون حريص وعطوف أكْتر هُوّ وعم بْيِتْعامل مع الطّبيعة ومخلوقاتا.

بِاللَّيْلِة اللي بَعْدا، خلَّصِت شهْرزاد قُصّةْ التّاجِر والجِنّي. كان المَلِك شهْرَيار مبْهور بِالْقِصّة هَيْدي وكان بدّو يِسمع كمان بعْد مِن القُصص الرّائِعة اللي شهْرزاد بِتِحْكِيا. وهيْك، ضلِّت شهْرزاد تِحْكي قُصصا للْملِك ليْلة بعْد ليْلة، وعلَّمِت الملِك وشعْبو دْروس مْهِمّة عن الحَياةْ والحِكْمة والعدِل.

## Questions

1. شو القُصّة اللي بلّشِت شهْرزاد تِحْكِيا بِاللّيْلِة التّانِية؟

2. ليْش الجِنّي عصّب مِن التّاجِر؟

3. شو طلب الجِنّي مِن التّاجِر يَعْمُل كِرمال يْسامْحو؟

4. مين الشّخِص اللي لقاه التّاجِر كِرمال يْساعْدو؟

5. كيف الرِّجّال الخِتْيار قنّع الجِنّي إنّو ما يِقْتُل التّاجِر؟

# Answers

1. بلّشِت شهْرزاد تِحْكي قُصّة التّاجِر والجِنّي العجيب.

2. عِصّب الجِنّي لِأنّو التّاجِر دمّر بَيْتو.

3. طلب الجِنّي مِن التّاجِر إنّو يْجيب حدا يِقْنعو إنّو ما يِقِتْلو.

4. التّاجِر لاقى زلمي خِتْيار حكيم كان يَعْرِف قُصص كْتير عن الجِنّ وعالمُن.

5. قنّع الرّجّال الخِتْيار الجِنّي إنّو ما يِقْتُل التّاجِر مِن وَرا إنّو خبّرو قُصّة مْشوّقة عن المُغامْرة والشّجاعة والتّضْحية، وبعْد ما الجِنّي سِمِع القُصّة، وافق إنّو يْسامِح التّاجِر ويْخلّيه يْعيش بِشرِط إنّو يِنْتِبِه وما يْعيد الغلْطة مرّة تانية.

## Chapter 2: The Genie and the Merchant

On the following night, King Shahryar asked Scheherazade to tell him a new story. Scheherazade began to narrate the tale of the merchant and the marvelous genie.

One day, a wealthy merchant went on a long journey to sell his goods. After a tiring journey, he stopped to rest under a tree. While he was sitting there, a giant and angry genie appeared.

The genie said to the merchant, "I will kill you because you destroyed my home." The merchant was frightened and did not understand what the genie meant. He asked the genie to explain the reason for his anger.

When you came and removed this wooden log to sit on it, some things fell on me and destroyed my small home where I lived.

The merchant was saddened by what had happened, but he did not know that there was a genie's home behind the tree. He asked the genie to show mercy and forgive him.

The genie said, "I will give you a chance to bring someone who can convince me not to kill you. If you fail, I will kill you for sure."

The merchant went on a long journey in search of someone to help him. Finally, he found a wise old man who knew a lot about genies and their world.

The old man listened to the merchant's story and decided to help him. They went together to the place of the tree where the genie was waiting for them.

The old man said to the genie, "I want to tell you a story before you decide the fate of this merchant. If you like the story, I hope you will forgive him and let him live."

The genie agreed to hear the story. The old man began to narrate an exciting tale of adventure, bravery, and sacrifice. The story was full of suspense and important lessons.

After hearing the story, the genie said, "I really liked the story and learned great lessons from it. I will forgive the merchant on the condition that he would be careful not to repeat such a mistake in the future."

The merchant thanked the genie for his mercy and promised to be more careful and compassionate in his actions. He also thanked the old man for his help and wisdom. Then, the merchant returned to his village and family and pledged to be more cautious and compassionate in his dealings with nature and its creatures.

On the following night, Scheherazade finished narrating the tale of the merchant and the genie. King Shahryar was impressed by this story and wanted to hear more wonderful stories told by Scheherazade. Thus, Scheherazade continued to narrate her stories to the king night after night, teaching him and his people important lessons about life, wisdom, and justice.

Questions
1. What is the story Scheherazade began to tell on the second night?
2. Why was the genie angry with the merchant?
3. What did the genie ask the merchant to do to forgive him?
4. Who did the merchant find to help him?
5. How did the old man convince the genie not to kill the merchant?

Answers
1. Scheherazade began to tell the story of the merchant and the strange genie.
2. The genie was angry because the merchant destroyed his home.
3. The genie asked the merchant to bring someone who could convince the genie not to kill him.
4. The merchant found a wise old man who knew a lot about genie and their world to help him.
5. The old man convinced the genie not to kill the merchant by telling an exciting story of adventure, bravery, and sacrifice. After hearing the story, the genie agreed to spare the merchant's life on the condition that he would be careful not to repeat such a mistake in the future.

# الفَصْل التّالِت
# الصِّيّاد والسَّمْكِة الذَّهبية

بِاللَّيْلِة اللي بعْدا، بلَّشِتْ شهْرزاد تْخبِّر قُصّة السَّمْكِة الذَّهبية والصَّيّاد لِلْملِك شهْريار.

كان في صيّاد فقير عايِش بِضيْعة بسيطة على البحر مع مرْتو. كان يِتْصيّاد السَّمك كِلّ يوْم كِرْمال يْعيِّش عيْلتو. وبيوْم مِن الإيّام، تْصيَّد سمْكة ذهبية حِلْوة كْتير كانِت بِتِلْمع قدّ ما حِلْوة.

حِكْيِت السَّمْكِة وقالِتْلو: "أنا سمْكِة سِحْرية، وإذا تركْتْني بْحقّقْلك تْلات أُمْنيّات بدّك ياها."

فكّر الصَّيّاد بِالشَّغْلات اللي هُوِّ مِحْتاجا وقرّر إنّو يُطْلُب مِن السَّمْكِة الذَّهبية تعْطي الثَّرْوِة والسَّعادِة والصِّحّة. فلّت السَّمْكِة وتْحقّقت أُمْنيّاتو.

حَياة الصَّيّاد ومرْتو تْحسّنِت كْتير مِن وَرا الأُمْنيات اللي حاقْتِلو ياهُن السّمْكِة الذَّهبية. بسّ مع مُرور الوَقِت، صارِت مرْتو تِطمع أكْتر، وطلبِت مِن جَوْزا إنّو يْروح للسَّمْكِة الذَّهبية ويُطْلُب بعْد أُمْنيّات.

رِجع الصَّيّاد للشّطّ، مطرح ما تصيّد السَّمْكِة الذَّهبية، وعيّطلا. طلّت السَّمْكِة مرّة تانية وسِمْعِت طلبات الصَّيّاد. بسّ هالمرّة حذَّرِتو السَّمْكِة إنّو الطَّمع مِش حَيْجِبْلو السَّعادِة والرّاحة.

تْعلَّم الصَّيّاد ومرْتو الدَّرْس المُهِمّ اللي السَّمْكِة حبّت تعْلّموه، وقرَّروا إنّو يِكْتِفوا بِاللّي معُن، ويْعيشوا حَياة بسيطة وسعيدة مِن دون طمع.

خلّصِت شهْرزاد قُصّة السّمْكِة الذّهبية والصّيّاد. كان المِلك شهْرَيار مُعْجب بِالْقُصّة هَيْدي وكان بدّو يِسْمع قُصص أكْتر فيا دْروس قيّمة وعِبر مْهِمّة.

وبِالطّريقة هَيْدي، ضلّت شهْرزاد تِحْكي قُصصا لِلْمِلك شهْرَيار ليْلِة بعْد ليْلِة، وعلّمِتو هُوّ وشعْبو دْروس مْهِمّة عن الرّضا والتّواضُع والسّعادِة.

## Questions

1. شو القُصّة اللي خبّرِتا شهْرزاد بِاللّيْلِة السّابْعة؟

2. شو تْصيّد الصّيّاد بِيوْم حظّو؟

3. شو قالِتو السّمْكِة الذّهبية للصّيّاد؟

4. شو الأُمْنِيات اللي طلبا الصّياد مِن السّمْكِة؟

5. كيف الصّيّاد ومرتو تْعلّموا الدّرس المْهِمّ اللي كانِت السّمْكِة الذّهبية بدّا تْعلّمُن ياه؟

## Answers

1. بلّشِت شهرزاد تْخبّر قُصّة السّمْكِة الذّهبية والصّيّاد.

2. تْصيّد الصّيّاد سمْكِة ذهبية حِلْوة كانِت بْتِلْمع قدّ ما حِلْوة.

3. قالِت السّمْكِة الذّهبية للصّيّاد إنّا سمْكِة سِحرية، وإنّو إذا ترَكا بِتْحقّقْلو تْلات أُمْنيّات بدّو ياها.

4. طلب الصّيّاد مِن السّمْكِة الذّهبية تعْطيه الثّروة والسّعادِة والصّحّة.

5. حذّرِت السّمْكِة الذّهبية الصّيّاد ومرْتو مِن إنّو الطّمع مِش حَيْجِبْلُن السّعادِة والرّاحة، تْعلّم الصّيّاد ومرْتو الدّرْس المْهِمّ وقرّروا إنّن يِكْتِفوا باللّى عِنْدُن ويْعيشوا حَياة بسيطة وسعيدِة مِن دون طمع.

# Chapter 3: The Fisherman and the Golden Fish

On the following night, Scheherazade began to tell the story of the Golden Fish and the Fisherman to King Shahryar.

There was a poor fisherman who lived in a simple coastal village with his wife. He fished every day to provide for his family. One day, he caught a beautiful golden fish that shimmered with brilliance and beauty. The fish spoke to him, saying, "I am a magical fish, and if you release me, I will grant you three wishes."

The fisherman thought about what he needed and decided to ask the golden fish to grant him wealth, happiness, and good health. He released the golden fish, and his wishes came true. The life of the fisherman and his wife improved greatly thanks to the wishes granted by the golden fish. But over time, his wife became greedy and asked her husband to return to the golden fish to ask for more wishes.

The fisherman returned to the beach, where he caught the golden fish and called out to it. The golden fish appeared again and listened to the fisherman's requests. But this time, the golden fish warned him that greed would not bring them happiness and peace.

The fisherman and his wife learned the valuable lesson that the golden fish wanted to teach them, and they decided to be content with what they had and live a simple and happy life without greed.

Scheherazade finished telling the story of the Golden Fish and the Fisherman. King Shahryar was impressed by this story and wanted to hear more stories that carry valuable lessons and important morals. In this way, Scheherazade continued to tell her stories to King Shahryar night after night, teaching him and his people important lessons about contentment, humility, and happiness.

Questions
1. What story did Scheherazade begin telling on the seventh night?
2. What did the fisherman catch on his lucky day?
3. What did the golden fish say to the fisherman?
4. What wishes did the fisherman ask the golden fish to grant him?
5. How did the fisherman and his wife learn the valuable lesson that the golden fish wanted to teach them?

Answers
1. Scheherazade began telling the story of the golden fish and the fisherman.
2. The fisherman caught a beautiful golden fish that sparkled with radiance and beauty.
3. The golden fish told the fisherman that it was a magical fish, and if he released it, it would grant him three wishes that he desired.

4. The fisherman asked the golden fish to grant him wealth, happiness, and good health.
5. The golden fish warned the fisherman and his wife that greed would not bring them happiness and peace. The fisherman and his wife learned a valuable lesson and decided to be content with what they had and live a simple and happy life without greed.

# الفصْل الرابِع
# علاء الدّين والمِصباح السِّحْري

بِاللّيْلِة اللي بعْدا، بلّشِتْ شهْرزاد تْخبّرْ قُصّةْ علاء الدّين والمِصْباح السِّحْري لِلْملِك شهْرَيار.

كان علاء الدّين ولَد فقير عايِش بِمدينِة صْغيرِة مع والِدتو. بِيوْم مِن الإيّام، قابل زلمي غريب قلّو إنّو هُوّ عمّو وعرض عليْه مُغامْرة إنّو يْنبْشوا فيا على كنْز مدفون. رُغِم مِن شُكوك علاء

الدّين، قرّر إنّو يِنضمّ للزّلمي الغريب بِرِحْلتو.

وُصلوا لمْغارة مْعتّمة، الكنْز كان مْخبّى فِيا. طلب الرِّجّال الغريب مِن علاء الدّين يْفوت عَ المْغارة وياخُد مِصباح قديم مَوْجود هونيك. بسّ بِمُجرّد ما علاء الدّين جاب المِصباح، سكّر الرِّجّال الغريب المْغارة وتركو محبوس جُوّا.

كِرمال يْجرّب يِضهر مِن المْغارة، صار علاء الدّين يْنبّش عَ طريق الضّهرة. لاقا المِصباح القديم وفكّر إنّو مُمْكِن يْضوّي بِالمْغارة المِعتْمة ويْنبّش على مخرج. بلّش علاء الدّين يْمسّح الغبرة عن المِصباح، وفجْأة ظهر جِنّي عِمْلاق. قال الجِنّي: "أنا جِنّي المِصباح السّحْري، وأنا هون كِرمال حقّق تْلات أُمْنِيّات بْتُطلُبا."

بْمُساعِدِة الجِنّي، قِدِر علاء الدّين يهْرُب مِن المْغارة ورجِع عَ المدينة. طلب مِن الجِنّي يْحقّق أُمْنِيّاتو: إنّو يْصير غني، ويِتْجوّز الأميرة ويْصير سُلْطان المدينة.

كِلّ أُمنِيّات علاء الدّين تْحقّقِت، وصار غني وتْجوّز الأميرة وتْولّى حُكم المدينة وصار السُّلطان. بسّ الزّلمي الغريب اللي كان بْيِدّعي إنّو عمّو كان عم بيخطّط كِرمال يِسرُق المِصباح السّحري ويِستخدِم قُوتو لَيتْحكّم بِالمدينة.

بِيوْم مِن الإيّام، قِدِر الرِّجّال الغريب يِسرُق المِصباح، وطلب مِن الجِنّي إنّو يِنقِل القصر اللي كان علاء الدّين والأميرة عايشين في لبلد بْعيد. حسّ علاء الدّين بِاليأس، بسّ تْذكّر خاتِم سِحري كان الرِّجّال الغريب عطاه ياه قبِل ما يْفوت عَ المغارة.

سْتخدم علاء الدّين الخاتِم السّحري كِرمال يِستدْعي جِنّي تاني كان بْيِخدمو. طلب مِن الجِنّي إنّو يْنقلو للقصِر ويْرِدّو عَ المدينة. بِمُساعْدِة الجِنّي والأميرة، قِدِر علاء الدّين يِسترْجِع المِصباح السّحْري ويْخسّر الرِّجّال الغريب.

رِجِع علاء الدّين لحَياتو كسُلْطان، وعاش سعيد مع الأميرة. تْعلّم علاء الدّين دْروس كْتيرة عن الثّقة والشّجاعة والحُبّ.

خلّصِت شهرزاد قُصّة علاء الدّين والمِصباح السّحْري. كان

المِلك شهْرَيار مُعْجب بِالْقّصة هَيْدي وكان بدّو يِسْمع كمان قُصص مُلِهْمة ومُشوّقة. وهيْك، ضلّت شهْرزاد تِحْكي قُصصا لِلْملِك شهْرَيار كِلّ ليْلِة، وتِعلْمو هُوِّ وشعْبو دْروس مْهِمّة عن الحَياةْ والحِكْمِة والعدِل.

## Questions

1. شو القُصّة اللي شهْرزاد خبّرِتا بِاللّيْلِة الرّابْعة؟

2. شو اللي عرضو الرِّجّال الغريب على علاء الدّين؟

3. شو لاقى علاء الدّين بِالِمْغارة؟

4. شو اللي عِمْلو الجِنّي اللي طِلِع مِن المِصْباح السِّحْري؟

5. شو الدْروس اللي تعلّما علاء الدّين مِن هَيْدي القُصّة؟

## Answers

1. بلّشِت شهْرزاد تِحْكي قُصّةْ علاء الدّين والمِصباح السِّحْري.

2. عرض الرِّجّال الغريب على علاء الدّين مُغامرة يْنبْشوا فِيا على كنْز مدْفون.

3. لِقي علاء الدّين مِصباح قديم جُوّا المْغارة.

4. قال الجِنّي إنّو جاهِز يْحقِّق تْلات أُمنِيّات بْيُطْلبا علاء الدّين.

5. تْعلّم علاء الدّين دْروس كْتيرِة عن الثِّقة والشّجاعة والحُبّ.

## Chapter 4: Aladdin and the Magic Lamp

On the next night, Scheherazade began to tell the story of Aladdin and the Magic Lamp to King Shahryar.

Aladdin was a poor boy who lived in a small city with his mother. One day, he met a strange man who claimed to be his uncle and offered him an adventure to search for a buried treasure. Despite Aladdin's suspicions, he decided to join the stranger on his journey.

They arrived at a dark cave where the treasure was hidden. The strange man asked Aladdin to enter the cave and take an old lamp that was there. But as soon as Aladdin got the lamp, the strange man closed the cave, trapping him inside.

In an attempt to get out of the cave, Aladdin started looking for a way out. He found the old lamp and thought it might be useful to light up the dark cave and to search for the exit. Aladdin started to wipe the dust off the lamp, and suddenly a giant genie appeared. The genie said, "I am the genie of the magic lamp, and I am here to grant three wishes that you make."

With the genie's help, Aladdin was able to escape from the cave and return to the city. He asked the genie to grant his wishes: to become rich, to marry the princess, and to become the sultan of the city.

All of Aladdin's wishes came true, and he became rich, married the princess, and became the sultan of the city. But the strange man who claimed to be his uncle was planning to steal the magic lamp and use its power to control the city.

One day, the strange man was able to steal the lamp and asked the genie to transport the palace where Aladdin and the princess lived to a distant land. Aladdin felt hopeless, but he remembered a magical ring that the strange man had given him before entering the cave.

Aladdin used the magical ring to summon another genie who served him. He asked the genie to transport him to the palace and return him to the city. With the help of the genie and the princess, Aladdin was able to retrieve the magic lamp and defeat the strange man.

Aladdin returned to his life as a sultan and lived happily with the princess. He learned many lessons about trust, courage, and love.

Scheherazade finished telling the story of Aladdin and the Magic Lamp. King Shahryar was impressed by this story and wanted to hear more inspiring and exciting stories. And so, Scheherazade continued to tell her stories to King Shahryar night after night, teaching him and his people important lessons about life, wisdom, and justice.

Questions
1. What story did Scheherazade begin telling on the fourth night?
2. What did the strange man offer Aladdin?
3. What did Aladdin find inside the cave?
4. What did the genie that came out of the magic lamp do?
5. What lessons did Aladdin learn from this story?

Answers
1. Scheherazade began telling the story of Aladdin and the Magic Lamp to King Shahryar.
2. The strange man offered Aladdin an adventure to search for a buried treasure.
3. Aladdin found an old lamp inside the cave.
4. The genie said he was there to grant three wishes that Aladdin requested.
5. Aladdin learned many lessons about trust, courage, and love.

# الفَصْل الخامِس
# علي بابا والأَرْبَعين حرامي

بِاللَّيلِة اللي بعْدا، بلّشِت شهْرزاد تْخبِّر للْمِلك شهْرَيار قُصَّةْ علي بابا والأَرْبَعين حرامي.

علي بابا كان زلمي بسيط عايِش بِضيْعة صْغيرِة وكان بْيِشْتِغِل حطّاب. بِيوْم مِن الإيّام، وهُوَّ بيقطّع الحطب بِالْغابِة، شاف مجْموعة مِن الحرامية فايْتين عَ مْغارة مِخْفية. قال زعيم

الحرامية كِلْمة سِرّية: "اِفْتح يا سِمْسِم"، نْفتحت البوّابِة الصّخْرية وفاتو الحرامية.

بسّ طِلْعوا الحرامية مِن المْغارة، راح علي بابا وقال الكِلْمة السِّرية كِرْمال يْفوت عَ المْغارة. لِقي الكنْز يَلّي الحرامية كانوا جمّعو وقرّر إنّو ياخُد جِزء مِنّو لَيْساعِد أهْلو وجيرانو.

عِرْفِت مَرْجانة، الخدّامِة الوَفية لعلي بابا، سِرّ الكنْز ومغارِةْ الحرامية. لمّا زعيم الحرامية عِرِف إنّو علي بابا كْتشف سِرُّن، قرّر إنّو يِنْتِقِم مِنّو ويْرجِّع الكنْز المسروق.

قاوَمِت مَرْجانة مُحاوَلات الحرامية إنّن يِقتْلوا علي بابا وعيْلتو، لحدّ ما قِدرِت بِالآخِر تِقْتل زعيم الحرامية وتنْقُذ علي بابا. سْتخدم علي بابا جِزء مِن الكنْز كِرْمال يْحسّن حَياتو هُوّ وعيْلتو ويْساعِد الفُقرا والمِحْتاجين بِالْقرْية.

خلّصِت شهْرزاد قُصّةْ علي بابا والأرْبْعين حرامي. كان الملِك شهْريار مبْهور بِالْقصّة وكان بدّو يِسمع قُصص كمان فِيا دْروس قيِّمة وعِبر مْهِمّة. وبِالطّريقة هَيْدي، ضلِّت شهْرزاد

تِحْكي قُصصا لِلْمِلِك شهْرَيار كِلّ ليْلِة، وتْعلُّمو هُوَّ وشعْبو دْروس مْهِمِّة عن الحَياةْ والشَّجاعة والصَّداقة.

## Questions

1. شو القُصّة اللي بلّشِت شهْرزاد تِحْكِيا بِاللّيْلِة الخامْسِة؟

2. شو المِهْنِة اللي كان علي بابا بْيِشْتِغِلا؟

3. شو الكِلْمة السّرّية اللي سْتخْدما زعيم الحرامية لَيِفْتح بوّابِةْ المْغارة؟

4. مين مُرْجانة وشو دَوْرا بِالْقُصّة؟

5. شو عِمِل علي بابا بِالْكنْز اللي لاقاه بِالمْغارة؟

## Answers

1. بلّشِت شهرزاد تْخبِّر قُصَّةْ علي بابا والأرْبَعين حرامي.

2. علي بابا كان بْيِشْتِغِل حطّاب.

3. الكِلْمة السِّرية اللي سْتَخْدما زَعيم الحرامية كانِت "اِفْتح يا سِمْسِم".

4. مُرْجانة هِيِّ الخدّامة الوَفية لِعلي بابا، عِرْفِت سِرّ الكنْز ومْغارِةْ الحرامية، وقاوِمِت مُحاوْلات الحرامية إنُّن يْقِتْلوا علي بابا وعيْلْتو، وبِالآخِر قِدْرِت تِقْتُل زَعيم الحرامية وتِنْقُذ علي بابا.

5. سْتخْدم علي بابا جِزِء مِن الكنْز لَيْحسِّن حَياتو هُوَّ وعيْلْتو ويْساعِد الفُقرا والمِحْتاجين بِالضّيْعة.

## Chapter 5: Ali Baba and the Forty Thieves

On the next night, Scheherazade began to tell the story of Ali Baba and the Forty Thieves to King Shahryar.
Ali Baba was a simple man who lived in a small village and worked as a woodcutter. One day while he was working in the forest, he saw a group of thieves entering a hidden cave. The leader of the thieves said a secret word, "Open Sesame," and the rock gate opened for them to enter.
After the thieves left the cave, Ali Baba went to the cave and said the secret word, entering the cave. He found the treasure that the thieves had collected and decided to take part of it to help his family and neighbors.
Morgiana, Ali Baba's loyal servant, learned about the treasure and the cave of the thieves. When the leader of the thieves learned that Ali Baba had discovered their secret, he decided to take revenge on him and get back the stolen treasure.
Morgiana fought against the attempts of the thieves to kill Ali Baba and his family until she finally managed to kill the leader of the thieves and save Ali Baba. Ali Baba used a part of the treasure to live a better life with his family and help the poor and needy in the village.
Scheherazade finished telling the story of Ali Baba and the Forty Thieves. King Shahryar was amazed by the story and wanted to hear more stories that carry valuable lessons and important messages. And so, Scheherazade continued to tell her stories to King Shahryar night after night, teaching him

and his people important lessons about life, courage, and friendship.

Questions
1. What is the story that Scheherazade began to tell on the fifth night?
2. What was Ali Baba's profession?
3. What was the secret word used by the leader of the thieves to open the cave gate?
4. Who is Morgiana, and what was her role in the story?
5. What did Ali Baba do with the treasure he found in the cave?

Answers
1. Scheherazade began to tell the story of Ali Baba and the Forty Thieves.
2. Ali Baba worked as a woodcutter.
3. The secret word used by the leader of the thieves was "Open Sesame."
4. Morgiana was Ali Baba's loyal servant. She discovered the secret of the treasure and the thieves' cave, and she foiled the attempts of the thieves to kill Ali Baba and his family. In the end, she managed to kill the leader of the thieves and save Ali Baba.
5. Ali Baba used part of the treasure to live a better life with his family and help the poor and needy in the village.

# الفَصْل السَّادِس
## الفِلَّاح الذَّكي والجِنّي الشَّقي

بِاللَّيْلِة السَّادْسِة، بلَّشِت شهْرزاد تِحْكي قُصَّة الفِلَّاح الذَّكي والجِنّي الشَّقي لِلْمِلِك شهْرَيار.

كان في فِلَّاح فقير بْيِشْتِغِل وبِيِتْعب كِرْمال يِكْسب لِقْمِة عيْشو. بِيوْم مِن الإيَّام، لاقى الفِلَّاح جرَّة نْحاس قديمِة مدْفونِة بِالْحقْلِة عِنْدو. قرَّر الفِلَّاح يِفْتح الجرَّة لَيْشوف شو فيا.

لمّا فتح الجرّة، طِلِع مِنّا جِنّي عِملاق، كان بدّو يِنْتِقِم مِن الفِلّاح لأنّو قلقْلو نَوْمتو الهادِية الطَّويلة. كان الجِنّي مُفكِّر إنّو الفِلّاح حَيُطْلُب مِنّو أُمْنية تَيْحسِّن حَياتو، بسّ الفِلّاح كان ذكي وعِمِل خُطّة لَيِتعامل مع الجِنّي.

قال الفِلّاح لِلْجِنّى إنّو مِش مُصدّق إنّو قَوي، وشايِف إنّو مِش حَيقْدر يرْجع عَ الجرّة. عصّب الجِنّي وحسّ بِالإهانة، فا قرّر يِثْبُت لِلْفِلّاح إنّو قوي ورِجع عَ الجرّة صُغري. لمّا رِجع الجِنّي عَ الجرّة، قفّل الفِلّاح الغطا هُوّ ومبْسوط.

وَعد الفِلّاح الجِنّي إنّو لح يْحرِّرو مرّة تاني إذا وَعدو إنّو ما بِأْذِ حدا وإنّو يُساعِد الفِلّاح وعيلْتو. قِبِل الجِنّي الشُّروط وتْعاون مع الفِلّاح، وتْحسّنِت حَياة الفِلّاح وعيلْتو بِفضل قُوّة الجِنّي وذكا الفِلّاح.

خلّصت شهْرزاد قُصّةْ الفِلّاح الذّكي والجِنّي الشّقي. كان المِلك شهْريار مُعْجب بِالْقِصّة هَيدي وبدّو يِسْمع قُصص أكْتر فِيا دْروس قيّمة وعِبر مُهِمّة عن الذّكاء والمكر والتّعاوُن بيْن البشر والجِنّ.

## Questions

1. شو القُصّة اللّي بلّشِت شهْرزاد تْخبّرا بِاللّيْلِة السّادْسِة؟

2. شو لِقي الفِلّاح بِالْحقْلِة عِنْدو؟

3. شو كان مْفكّر الجِنّي لمّا الفلّاح ضهّرو؟

4. شو الخُطّة اللي عِمِلا الفِلّاح كِرْمال يِتْعامل مع الجِنّي؟

5. كيف تْحسّنِت حَياة الفِلّاح وعيلْتو؟

# Answers

1. بلّشِت شهْرزاد تِحْكي قُصّةْ الفِلّاح الذّكي والجِنّي الشّقي.

2. لِقي الفِلّاح جرّةْ نْحاس قديمِة مدْفونِة بِالْحقْلِة عِنْدو.

3. كان الجِنّي مْفكّر إنّو الفِلّاح حَيُطْلُب مِنّو أُمْنِية كِرْمال يْحسّن حَياتو.

4. قال الفِلّاح لِلْجِنّي إنّو مِش مْصدّق إنّو قَوي وشايِف إنّو مِش حَيقْدر يِرْجع مرّة تانْية عَ الجرّة. عَصَب الجِنّي وحسّ بِالإهانِة، فا قرّر يِثْبُت لِلْفِلّاح إنّو قَوي ورِجِع عَ الجرّة صُغري. لمّا رِجِع الجِنّي لِلْجرّة، قفّل الفِلّاح الغطا هُوّ ومبْسوط.

5. تْحسّنِت حَياة الفِلّاح وعيلْتو بِفضل قُوّة الجِنّي وذكا الفِلّاح، بَعْد ما وَعدو الجِنّي إنّو ما يِئْذي حدا، وإنّو يْساعِد الفِلّاح وعيلْتو.

## Chapter 6: The Clever Farmer and the Mischievous Genie

On the sixth night, Scheherazade began to tell the story of the Clever Farmer and the Mischievous Genie to King Shahryar.

There was a poor farmer who worked hard to provide for his family. One day, he found an old copper vessel buried in his field. The farmer decided to open the vessel to see what was inside.

As soon as he opened the vessel, a giant genie emerged from it, seeking revenge on the farmer for interrupting his long slumber. The genie thought the farmer would ask for a wish to improve his life, but the farmer was clever and had a plan to deal with the genie.

The farmer told the genie that he did not believe in his power and did not think he could return to the vessel. The genie felt angry and humiliated, so he decided to prove his power to the farmer and immediately returned to the vessel. Once the genie was back in the vessel, the farmer closed the lid with joy.

The farmer promised to release the genie again if he promised not to harm anyone and to help the farmer and his family. The genie agreed to the conditions and cooperated with the farmer, and the life of the farmer and his family improved thanks to the genie's power and the farmer's cleverness.

Scheherazade finished telling the story of the Clever Farmer and the Mischievous Genie. King Shahryar was impressed by this story and wanted to hear more stories that carry valuable lessons and important morals about intelligence, cunning, and cooperation between humans and genies.

Questions
1. What is the story that Scheherazade began to tell on the sixth night?
2. What did the farmer find in his field?
3. What did the genie think when the farmer released him?
4. What was the plan the farmer had to deal with the genie?
5. How did the life of the farmer and his family improve?

Answers
1. Scheherazade began to tell the story of the Clever Farmer and the Mischievous Genie.
2. The farmer found an old brass vessel buried in his field.
3. The genie thought the farmer would ask for a wish to improve his life.
4. The farmer told the genie that he did not believe in his power and did not think he could return to the vessel. The genie felt angry and humiliated, so he decided to prove his power to the farmer and immediately

returned to the vessel. Once the genie was back in the vessel, the farmer closed the lid with joy.

5. The life of the farmer and his family improved thanks to the genie's power and the farmer's cleverness after the genie promised not to harm anyone and to help the farmer and his family.

# الفصل السّابع
# حرامي إسكنْدرية ورئيس الشُّرطة

بِليْلِة مِن لَيالي شهرزاد، بلّشِتْ تِحْكي عن قُصّةْ حرامي إسْكنْدرية ورئيس الشُّرطة.

بِمدينةْ إسْكنْدرية الحِلْوة، كان في حرامي ذكي وشاطِر بْيِسْرُق مِن الأغْنيا وبيوَزِّع على الفُقرا. كِلّ النّاس كانوا بْيِحْكوا عن الحرامي هَيْدا لإنّو ما حدا قِدِر يْمِسْكو. قرّر رئيس الشُّرطة إنّو

يِمْسُك الحرامي هَيدا ويْوَقِّف جرايْمو.

فكّر رئيس الشُّرطة بِخطّة ذكية كِرْمال يِقْبِض على الحرامي. نْتشرِت إشاعة عن كنْز كْبير حيِنْقل بِالمدينة. الإشاعة هَيدي كانِت مُجرّد فخّ كِرْمال بِجذُب الحرامي.

بِاللّيْلة المْحدِّدِة، نطر رئيس الشُّرطة ورْجالو بِكمين كِرْمال يِلْقطوا الحرامي. وفِعْلاً، بيّن الحرامي وجرّب يِسْرُق الكنْز الوَهْمي. هجم عْليْه رئيس الشُّرطة ورْجالو وقبضو عْليْه.

بسّ الحرامي ما سْتسْلم بِسْهولِة، وقِدِر إنّو يِفْلِت مِن الحِصار وهرب بِالزّواريب المْعتِّمة. بلّشِت مُطارِدة مُثيرة بين الحرامي ورئيس الشُّرطة بِالْمدينة. بِالآخِر، نِجِح رئيس الشُّرطة إنّو يِمْسُك الحرامي وقبض عْليْه.

و رغِم إنّو نْلقط عَ الحرامي، بسّ رئيس الشُّرطة كان بْيِعْترِف بِذكا وشجاعِة الحرامي. وبِالْمحكمة، قرّر القاضي إنّو يَعْطي الحرامي فُرْصة يْغيِّر حَياتو بِإنّو يِشْتِغِل عِند رئيس الشُّرطة

كِرْمال يْحارِب الجريمِة.

و هيْك خُلْصِت قُصّةْ حرامي إسْكنْدرية ورئيس الشُّرْطة، إللى علّمتْنا إنّو الذّكا والشّجاعة مُمْكِن يُسْتخْدموا لِلْخيْر.

## Questions

1. حرامي إسْكنْدرية شو كان يَعْمُل بعْد ما بِسْرق مِن الأغْنيا؟

2. شو قرّر رئيس الشُّرطة يَعْمُل كِرْمال يِلْقط الحرامي؟

3. شو صار لمّا الحرامي جرّب يِسرُق الكنْز الوَهْمي؟

4. كيف الحرامي قِدِر يِهْرُب مِن الحِصار؟

5. شو قرّر القاضى يَعْمُل بِالحرامي بعْد ما نْقبض علَيْه؟

## Answers

1. حرامي إسْكنْدرية كان يْوَزِّع اللي سرقو مِن الأغْنيا على الفُقرا.

2. قرّر رئيس الشُّرطة إنّو يَعْمُل خُطّة ذكية كِرْمال يُقْبُض على الحرامي، وهِيِّ نشر إشاعة عن كنز كْبير حَيِتْنقل بِالْمدينة، وكانِت الإشاعة هَيْدي فخّ كِرْمال يِجْذُب الحرامي.

3. لمّا الحرامي جرّب يِسرُق الكنْز الوَهْمي، هجم عْليْه رئيس الشُّرْطة ورْجالو وقبضوا عليْه.

4. قِدِر الحرامي يِهرُب مِن الحِصار مِن وَرا إنّو ما سْتسْلم بِسْهولِة وهرب بِالزَّواريب المِعتْمِة.

5. قرّر القاضي يَعْطي الحرامي فُرصة يْغيِّر حَياتو بِإنّو يِشْتِغِل عِند رئيس الشُّرْطة كِرْمال يْقاوِم الجريمة.

## Chapter 7: The Thief of Alexandria and the Police Chief

During one of Shahrazad's nights, she began to tell the story of the Thief of Alexandria and the Police Chief.

In the beautiful city of Alexandria, there was a clever and skilled thief who stole from the rich and gave to the poor. Everyone was talking about this thief because no one could catch him. The police chief decided to catch this thief and put an end to his crimes.

The police chief thought of a clever plan to capture the thief. A rumor spread about a huge treasure that would be transported through the city. This rumor was just a trap to lure the thief.

On the designated night, the police chief and his men waited in ambush to catch the thief. And indeed, the thief appeared and tried to steal the imaginary treasure. The police chief pounced on him and caught him.

But the thief did not surrender easily. He managed to escape the grip and fled into one of the dark alleys. An exciting chase began between the thief and the police chief throughout the city. In the end, the police chief managed to catch the thief and arrested him.

Despite the arrest of the thief, the police chief recognized his intelligence and courage. In court, the judge decided to give the thief a chance to change his life and work under the police chief to fight crime.

And so, the story of the Thief of Alexandria and the Police Chief ended, teaching us that intelligence and courage can be used for good.

Questions
1. What did the Thief of Alexandria do after stealing from the rich?
2. What did the police chief decide to do to catch the thief?
3. What happened when the thief tried to steal the imaginary treasure?
4. How did the thief manage to escape the grip?
5. What did the judge decide about the thief after his arrest?

Answers
1. The Thief of Alexandria distributed what he stole from the rich to the poor.
2. The police chief decided on a clever plan to catch the thief, which was to spread a rumor about a huge treasure that would be transported through the city, considering this rumor a trap to lure the thief.
3. When the thief tried to steal the imaginary treasure, the police chief and his men pounced on him and caught him.

4. The thief managed to escape the grip by not surrendering easily and fleeing into one of the dark alleys.
5. The judge decided to give the thief a chance to change his life and work under the police chief to fight crime.

# الفَصْل التّامِن
# العُصْفور الأَزْرق

بِاللَّيْلِة اللي بعْدا، بلّشِت شهْرزاد تِحْكي لِلْمِلك شهْريار حْكايِةْ العصْفور الأزْرق.

كان في عصْفور أزْرق نادِر وحِلو عايِش بغابِة سِحْرية بْعيدِة. كان النّاس بيقولوا إنّو العصْفور الأزْرق هَيْدا بْيِقْدر يْجيب السّعادِة والحظّ السّعيد لَيّلي بيلاقيه. في أميرة صبية سِمْعِت

عن العصفور الأزرق وقرّرت تْنبّش عليه كِرمال تْحقّق السّعادة لمَمْلِكِتا وشعْبا.

بلّشِت الأميرة رِحْلِة طَويلة ومُغامْرة شيّقة كِرمال تْنبّش على العصفور الأزرق. وبالرّحْلة هَيْدي، قابلت رِفقات كْتير وحَيَوانات مِتعاوْنة ساعِدِتا إنّا تِقْطع كِلّ الصّعوبات والتّحدّيّات.

بعْد سِلْسِلِة طَويلِة مِن التّحدِيّات والمُغامرات، لاقِت الأميرة العصْفور الأزْرق. بسّ بدل ما يْجيبْلا السّعادِة صُغْري، علّما العصْفور إنّو السّعادِة الحقيقية بْتيجي مِن الشّغِل بِاجْتِهاد، ومُواجْهِةْ المشاكِل والتّحدِيّات بِشجاعة وعزيمة.

رِجْعِت الأميرة لمَمْلِكِتا وقالِت لشعْبا الحِكْمة القِيِّمة اللي تْعلِّمتا مِن العصفور الأزْرق. تْحسّنِت حَياة النّاس بِالمَمْلِكة وزادِت سعادِتُن، وهيْك حقّقِت الأميرة هدفا مِن خِلال الشّغِل بِالاجْتِهاد والتّعاوُن مع شعْبا بدل ما تِعْتِمد على قُوة سِحْرية.

خلّصِت شهْرزاد خبْرية العصْفور الأزْرق. كان الملِك شهْريار مبْهور بِالْحْكايِة وبدّو يِسمع قُصص أكْتر فِيا دُروس قيِّمة وعِبر مْهِمّة.
وبِالطّريقة هَيْدي، ضلِّت شهْرزاد بإنّا تِحْكي لِلْمِلك شهْريار حْكايِة وَرا حْكايِة، وتعلّمو هُوّ وشعْبو دُروس مْهِمّة عن الشّغِل بِجِهْد ومُواجْهِة التّحْدِيّات بِشجاعة وعزيمِة.

## Questions

1. شو هِيِّ القُصّة اللي بلّشِت شهْرزاد تْخبّرا بِاللّيْلِة التّامِنِة؟

2. شو القِدْرة السِّحْرية اللي عنْدو ياها العصْفور الأزْرق؟

3. ليْش قرّرِت الأميرة تْنبّش على العصْفور الأزْرق؟

4. شو الدّرْس المْهِمّ اللي تْعلّمتو الأميرة مِن العصْفور الأزْرق؟

5. كيف تْحسّنِت حَياةْ النّاس بِالمْملكِة بعْد ما رِجْعِت الأميرة؟

# Answers

1. بلّشِت شهرزاد تِحْكي قُصّةْ العصفورْ الأزْرق.

2. العصْفور الأزْرق بْيِمْتِلِك القُدْرة على إنّو يْخلّي النّاس سُعداء وبِيْجيب الحظّ السّعيد لَيَلّي بْيِقْدر يْلاقيه.

3. قرّرت الأميرة تْنبّش على العصفور الأزْرق كِرْمال تْحقّق السّعادِة لِممْلِكِتا وشعْبا.

4. تعلّمت الأميرة مِن العصفور الأزْرق إنّو السّعادِة الحقيقية بْتيجي مِن الشّغِل بِجهْد ومُواجْهةْ المشاكِل والتّحدِيّات بِشجاعة وعزيمة.

5. تْحسّنِت حَياةْ النّاس بِالْممْلِكة وزادِت سعادِتُن بعْد ما عرّفِت الأميرة شعْبا الدّرْس الْمِهمّ اللي تْعلّمِتو مِن العصفور الأزْرق، وحقّقِت هدفا مِن خِلال الشّغِل بِاجْتِهاد والتّعاوُن مع شعْبا بدل ما تِعْتِمد على قُوة سِحْرِية.

# Chapter 8: The Blue Bird

On the following night, Scheherazade began telling the story of the Blue Bird to King Shahryar.

There was a rare and beautiful blue bird that lived in a distant magical forest. It was said that the blue bird had the ability to grant happiness and good luck to those who could find it. A young princess heard about the Blue Bird and decided to search for it to bring happiness to her kingdom and its people.

The princess embarked on a long and exciting adventure to find the Blue Bird. She met, on her journey, many friends and helpful animals who helped her overcome obstacles and challenges.

After a long series of challenges and adventures, the princess finally found the Blue Bird. But instead of giving her happiness directly, the Blue Bird taught her that true happiness comes from hard work and facing problems and challenges with courage and determination.

The princess returned to her kingdom and shared the valuable lesson she learned from the Blue Bird with her people. Their lives improved, and their happiness increased. The princess had achieved her goal through hard work and cooperation with her people instead of relying on magical powers.

Scheherazade finished telling the story of the Blue Bird. King Shahryar was amazed by the story and wanted to hear more stories that carry valuable lessons and important morals. And so, Scheherazade continued to tell her stories to King Shahryar night after night, teaching him and his people important lessons about hard work and facing challenges with courage and determination.

Questions
1. What story did Scheherazade begin telling on the eighth night?
2. What magical ability does the Blue Bird have?
3. Why did the princess decide to search for the Blue Bird?
4. What valuable lesson did the princess learn from the Blue Bird?
5. How did people's lives improve in the kingdom after the princess's return?

Answers
1. Scheherazade began telling the story of the Blue Bird.
2. The Blue Bird has the ability to grant happiness and good luck to those who can find it.
3. The princess decided to search for the Blue Bird to bring happiness to her kingdom and its people.
4. The princess learned from the Blue Bird that true happiness comes from hard work and facing problems and challenges with courage and determination.

5. People's lives in the kingdom improved, and their happiness increased after the princess shared the valuable lesson she learned from the Blue Bird and achieved her goal through hard work and cooperation with her people instead of relying on magical powers.

# الفصْل التّاسِع
## البِنْت والسّاحْرة الخْتْيارة

بِاللّيْلِة اللي بعْدا، بلّشِت شهْرزاد تِحْكي لِلْمِلِك شهْرَيار عن قُصّة البِنْت والسّاحْرة الخِتْيارة.

كان في بِنْت صبية عايْشِة مع أُمّا بِضيْعة صْغيرِة. كانِت البِنْت بِتعاني مِن الفقْر والجوع. بيوْم مِن الإيّام، لاقِت سِت خِتْيارة بِتْبيع وَرد بِالسّوق. شْترِت البِنْت وَرْدِة مِن السّتّ

الخِتْيارة بالْمصاري القليلة اللي كانِت معا.

ضِحْكِت السِّتّ الخِتْيارة وشكرِت البِنت على لُطفا. قالِتْلا إنّا ساحْرة وعرضِت عليا تْحقِّقْلا أُمْنِية وحْدِة. فكّرِت البِنت باللي هيِّ بدّا ياه وقرّرِت تُطلُب مِن السّاحْرة الخِتْيارة تَعْطِيا القُدْرة على إنّا تْخلّي النّاس اللي حَواليا مبْسوطين.

قِبْلِت السّاحْرة الخِتْيارة إنّا تعْطي البِنت الهِبة اللي طلبِتا. بلّشِت البِنت تِسْتعْمِل القُدْرة هَيْدي كِرْمال تْفرِّح النّاس بِضيْعِتا. مع الوَقِت، نْشهرِت البِنت وصارِت محبوبة والكِلّ بيقدِّرا.

خلّصِت شهرزاد قُصّة البِنت والسّاحْرة الخِتْيارة. كان المِلِك شهرْيار مُعْجب بِالْقُصّة هَيْدي وحبّ يِسْمع قُصص تانْية فيا دْروس قيِّمة وعِبر مْهِمّة عن الإحْسان والتّفاني بِخِدْمِة النّاس. وهيْك، ضلّت شهرزاد تِحْكي قُصصا لِلْمِلِك شهرْيار كِلّ ليْلة

وتْعلّمو هُوَّ وشعْبو دْروس مُهِمَّة عن التّضْحية والتّفاني بِمُساعْدِة النّاس وتحْقيق السّعادة للْكِلّ.

## Questions

1. شو القُصّة اللي بلّشِت شهرزاد تْخبّرا بِاللّيْلة التّاسعة؟

2. شو كانِت السّتّ الخِتْيارة بِتْبيع بِالسّوق؟

3. شو طلبِت البِنْت مِن السّاحْرة الخِتْيارة؟

4. كيف الهِبة اللي السّاحْرة الخِتْيارة عطِتا للبِنْت أثّرِت على حَياتا؟

5. شو الدُّروس المِهِمّة اللي علّمِتا شهْرزاد لِلمِلِك شهْرَيار وشعْبو مِن خِلال القُصّة هَيْدي؟

## Answers

1. بلّشِت شهْرزاد تِحْكي قُصَّة البِنْت والسّاحْرة الخِتْيارة.

2. السّتّ الخِتْيارة كانِت بِتْبيع وَرد بالسّوق.

3. طلبِت البِنْت مِن السّاحْرة الخِتْيارة إنّا تعْطِيا القُدْرة على إنّا تْخلّي النّاس اللي حوالَيا مبْسوطين.

4. بلّشِت البِنْت تِسْتخْدِم القُدْرة هَيْدي كِرْمال تْفرّح النّاس بِضيْعِتا، ومع الوَقِت، نْشهْرِت البِنْت وصارِت محبوبِة والكِلّ بيْقِدرا.

5. علّمِت شهْرزاد المِلِك شهْرَيار وشعْبو دْروس مْهِمّة عن التّضْحية والتّفاني بِمُساعْدِة النّاس وتِحْقيق السّعادِة للكِلّ.

## Chapter 9: The Girl and the Magical Old Woman

On the following night, Scheherazade began telling the story of the Girl and the Magical Old Woman to King Shahryar.

There was a young girl who lived with her mother in a small village. The girl suffered from poverty and hunger. One day, she stumbled upon an old woman selling flowers in the market. The girl bought a flower from the old woman with the little money she had.

The old woman smiled and thanked the girl for her kindness. She revealed that she was a sorceress and offered to grant the girl one wish. The girl thought about what she wanted and decided to ask the magical old woman to give her the ability to make people around her happy.

The magical old woman granted the girl the gift she asked for. The girl began using this ability to make people in her village happy. With time, the girl's fame spread, and she became beloved and honored by everyone.

Scheherazade finished telling the story of the Girl and the Magical Old Woman. King Shahryar was impressed by this story and wanted to hear stories that carried valuable lessons and important morals about kindness and dedication to serving others. And so, Scheherazade continued to tell her stories to King Shahryar night after night, teaching him and his people important lessons about generosity and selflessness to help others and achieve happiness for all.

Questions
1. What story did Scheherazade start telling on the ninth night?
2. What was the old woman selling in the market?
3. What did the girl ask the magical old woman for?
4. How did the gift given to the girl by the magical old woman affect her life?
5. What important lessons did Scheherazade teach King Shahryar and his people through this story?

Answers
1. Scheherazade started telling the story of the girl and the magical old woman.
2. The old woman was selling flowers in the market.
3. The girl asked the magical old woman to grant her the ability to make people around her happy.
4. The girl began using this ability to make people happy in her village, and over time, her fame spread, and she became loved and honored by everyone.
5. Scheherazade taught King Shahryar and his people important lessons about sacrifice and selflessness in helping others and achieving happiness for all.

# الفصل العاشِر
# الأمير والتِّنين

بِاللّيْلِة اللي بعْدا، بلّشِت شهْرزاد تِحْكي قُصّةْ الأمير والتِّنين لِلْملِك شهْريار.

كان في أمير شبّ وشُجاع عايِش بِممْلكِة بْعيدِة. نْتشر بِالْبلد خبر إنّو في تِنين عِمْلاق عايِش بِجبل قريب، عم بيهدّدّ الضِّيَع القريبِة وعم بيخوّف النّاس. قرّر الأمير إنّو يْواجِهْ التِّنين

ويْخلِّص شعْبو مِن الخطر.

جهّز الأمير حالو للمعْركة وتّجهْ عَ الجبل. لمّا قابل الأمير التّنين، كْتشف إنّو مِش شِرّير مِتل ما كان النّاس مْفكّرين. التّنين كان عم بيسبّب دمار لأنّو كان حاسِس بِوَجع بِجسْمو. عرض الأمير إنّو يْساعِد التّنين ويْعالِج وَجعو بِشرْط إنّو يْوَعدو ما يِئْذي النّاس مرّة تانْية.

وافق التّنين على المطلوب والأمير ساعدو. بعْد ما صحّ التّنين، عاش هُوّ والأمير بِسلام وصداقة، وتْعاونوا بِحِمايِة الضّيَع والبلد مِن الأعْداء والخطر.

خلّصِت شهْرزاد قِصّةْ الأمير والتّنين. كان الملِك شهْرَيار مبْهور بِالْقِصّة، وحبّ يِسْمع قُصص أكْتر فِيا دْروس قيِّمة ومعاني مْهِمّة عن الصّداقة والتّفاهُم بيْن المخْلوقات المُخْتلِفة.

و هيْك، ضلّت شهْرزاد تِحْكي قُصصا مِلْيانة عِبر وحِكم

لِلْمِلِك شهْرَيار كِلّ لَيْلِة. تْأثَّر المِلِك كْتير بِكلام شهْرزاد ودْروسا القيِّمة، وتْغيَّرِت نظْرِتو لِلْحَياة والعالم حَوالَيْه.

و بِفضْل حِكْمِة شهْرزاد وقُدْرِتا على التّواصُل ونقْل العِبر والدُّروس القيِّمة عن طريق قُصصا، المِلِك شهْرَيار صار مِلِك حكيم وعادِل. رجّع السّلام والنّجاح لِممْلكْتو وحكم بِحِكْمِة ورحْمِة ما شافا الشّعْب مِن قبِل.

بِمُرور الزّمن، كْتشف المِلِك شهْرَيار إنّو لِقي بِشهْرزاد الزّوْجِة الحكيمة والمُخْلِصة. صارِت شهْرزاد مِلِكة محبوبِة مِن الشّعْب وإمّ لِلأميرة الصّغيرِة.

ضلِّت شهْرزاد تِحْكي القُصص لِلْمِلِك كِلّ لَيْلِة، وهَيْدا خلّاه يْقدِّرا ويِحْتِرما أكْتر وأكْتر. وعاش المِلِك شهْرَيار وشهْرزاد مبْسوطين مع بعْض، وضلِّت قُصصا تُنْشُر الحِكْمة والمعْرِفة بِكِلّ المَمْلكِة.

و هيْك، ضلِّت شهْرزاد تألِّف قُصص مُثيرة ورائِعة لِلْمِلِك شهْرَيار لَيْلِة بعْد لَيْلِة، وضلّوا يِتْعلَّموا مِن دُروسا وعجائِبا. ضلِّت المَمْلكِة تِزْدِهِر تحِت حِكْمِة وسعادِة شهْرزاد وشهْرَيار،

وصارِت قُصص ألْف ليْلِة وليلِة مصْدر إلْهام للنّاس بِكلّ أنْحاء العالم.

## Questions

1. شو القُصّة اللي شهرزاد بلّشِت تخبّرا بِاللّيْلِة العاشْرة؟

2. شو هُوّ الخبر اللي نْتشر عن التّنين اللي عايِش بِالْجبل؟

3. شو كْتشف الأمير لمّا قابل التّنين؟

4. شو الاِتّفاق اللي عِملو الأمير مع التّنين؟

5. كيف قُصص شهرزاد أثّرِت على المِلك شهرَيار ومَمْلِكْتو؟

## Answers

1. بلّشِت شهرزاد تِحْكي قُصّة الأمير والتّنين.

2. نْتشر خبر عن تِنين كْبير عايِش بِجبل قريب، عم بيهدّد الضّيَع القريبِة وعم بيخوّف النّاس.

3. كْتشف الأمير إنّو التّنين مِش شِرّير مِتل ما كان النّاس مْفكّرين، بس التّنين كان عم بيسبّب دمار لأنّو كان حاسِس بْوَجع بْجِسْمو.

4. عرض الأمير إنّو يْساعِد التّنين ويْعالِج وَجعو بِشرط إنّو يْوَعْدو ما يِئْذي النّاس مرّة تانْية. ووافق التّنين على الاِتّفاق هَيْدا.

5. تأثّر المَلِك شهْريار بِشكِل عميق بِكلام شهرزاد وعِبرا القيّمة، وتْغيّرِت نظْرتو لِلْحَياة والعالم مِن حَوالَيْه. صار ملِك حكيم وعادِل ورجّع السّلام والاِزْدِهار لمَمْلكْتو. تْعلّم شعْبو مِن العِبر والدّروس القيّمة اللي مَوْجودِة بِقُصص شهرزاد، وزْدهرِت المَمْلكِة وعاش شعْبا بِسلام وسعادِة.

# Chapter 10: The Prince and the Dragon

On the next night, Scheherazade began telling the story of the Prince and the Dragon to King Shahryar.

There was a young and brave prince who lived in a distant kingdom. News spread in the land about a huge dragon living in a nearby mountain, threatening the neighboring villages and scaring people. The prince decided to face the dragon and save his people from danger.

The prince prepared for the battle and headed to the mountain. When he faced the dragon, he discovered that the dragon was not evil as everyone thought. Rather, he caused destruction because of pain in his body. The prince offered to help the dragon to heal his pain in exchange for a promise not to harm people again.

The dragon agreed to the deal, and the prince helped him. After the dragon healed, the prince and the dragon lived in peace and friendship, and they cooperated to protect the villages and the country from enemies and risks.

Scheherazade finished narrating the story of the Prince and the Dragon. King Shahryar was impressed by this story and wanted to hear more stories that carry valuable lessons and important messages about friendship and understanding between different creatures.

And so, Scheherazade continued to tell her stories filled with lessons and wisdom to King Shahryar every night. King Shahryar was deeply affected by Scheherazade's words and valuable messages, and his view of life and the world around him changed.

Thanks to Scheherazade's wisdom and her ability to communicate and convey valuable lessons and messages through her stories, King Shahryar became a wise and just king. He restored peace and prosperity to his kingdom and ruled with wisdom and mercy that the people had not seen before.

Over time, King Shahryar realized that he had found in Scheherazade a wise and loyal wife. Scheherazade became a beloved queen to the people and a mother to the little princess.

Scheherazade continued to tell stories to the king every night, making him appreciate and respect her more and more. King Shahryar and Scheherazade lived happily together as her stories continued to spread wisdom and knowledge throughout the kingdom.

And thus, Scheherazade continued to weave her thrilling and wonderful stories for King Shahryar night after night, learning from them and teaching him with her lessons and marvels. The kingdom thrived under the wisdom and happiness of Scheherazade and Shahryar, while the tales of One Thousand and One Nights inspired people all over the world.

Questions
1. What was the story that Scheherazade began telling on the tenth night?
2. What rumor spread about the dragon living in the mountain?
3. What did the prince discover when he faced the dragon?
4. What agreement did the prince make with the dragon?
5. How did Scheherazade's stories affect King Shahryar and his kingdom?

Answers
1. Scheherazade began telling the story of the Prince and the Dragon.
2. Rumors spread in the land about a huge dragon living in a nearby mountain, threatening the neighboring villages and scaring people.
3. The prince discovered that the dragon was not evil as everyone thought. Rather, he caused destruction because of pain in his body.
4. The prince offered to help the dragon to heal his pain in exchange for a promise not to harm people again, and the dragon agreed to the agreement.
5. King Shahryar was deeply affected by Scheherazade's words and valuable messages, and his view of life and the world around him changed. He became a wise and just king who restored peace and prosperity to his

kingdom. The people learned from the lessons and valuable messages carried by Scheherazade's stories, and the kingdom prospered, and its people lived in peace and happiness.

# lingualism

*Visit our website for information on current and upcoming titles and free language learning resources.*

# www.lingualism.com

www.ingramcontent.com/pod-product-compliance
Lightning Source LLC
Chambersburg PA
CBHW052121070526
44586CB00016B/2028